MW00811568

PRAYER JOURNAL

THIS JOURNAL BELONGS TO:

___

**EVERY MOMENT HOLY:
PRAYER JOURNAL**

Rabbit Room Press
3321 Stephens Hill Lane
Nashville, TN 37013
info@rabbitroom.com

EDITORS
Hannah Hubin
& Douglas Kaine McKelvey

DEVELOPED BY
Leslie Eiler Thompson
& Hannah Hubin

(Brown) ISBN 9781951872502
(Grey) ISBN 9781951872199
Printed in China

EVERY *moment* HOLY

PRAYER JOURNAL

RABBIT ROOM
PRESS

CONTENTS

How to Use This Journal

THIS PRAYER JOURNAL CONSISTS OF fifty-two entries. Each entry includes a portion of a liturgy from *Every Moment Holy: Volume I* paired with two passages of scripture and three journal-response prompts. These prompts are intended to guide you toward:

- Cultivating an awareness of God's presence in a particular moment or season as you engage in conversation with your Maker, naming and giving honest expression to your thoughts, feelings, fears, and hopes

- Remembrance of the Lord's faithful presence in similar past moments

- A meditation on the truths of scripture as an anchor and a reminder that this moment sits in the greater context of the entire history of redemption—past, present, and future—and that, regardless of our current emotions or worries, God's promises to us remain true

- Surrender to the workings of the Spirit unto the end that—even through these circumstances—your own heart might be more conformed to the heart of Christ, and that you might be moved toward a deeper life of doxology—praise, worship, and thanksgiving.

Each entry also includes a blank page on which you might pen an original prayer of response in your own words, or capture additional thoughts and notes.

Our intention is to offer, through the fifty-two topics in this journal, a varied cross-section of the ever-changing seasons of the human soul as it navigates seasons of grief, celebration, joy, disappointment, worry, hope, and wonder alike.

Some journal users might opt to work through these fifty-two topics in a year's time, at a pace of one entry per week. Others will doubtless find it helpful to utilize the journal more frequently or more sporadically. You might ignore some topics but return often to others, working through them repeatedly.

No matter how you choose use it, there is no prescribed pace or order in which you should engage with these prayerful meditations. Our hope is that, however you incorporate this journal into the rhythms of your life, you will find it useful as a sort of spiritual atlas, allowing you to better map the current location of your heart and inviting you to engage more meaningfully with your Creator.

We also hope that in future years this journal might become for you a written witness to look back on—a chronicle of your own spiritual journey and of the movement of God's mercy, kindness, grace, and love faithfully extended to you over time, meeting you again and again so that you might proclaim along with the Apostle Paul this great truth:

> For I am convinced that neither death nor life, neither angels nor demons, neither the present nor the future, nor any powers, neither height nor depth, nor anything else in all creation, will be able to separate us from the love of God that is in Christ Jesus our Lord.
>
> —Romans 8:38–39

Now may the grace and peace of
God rest upon you—
across all seasons,
through any circumstance,
in every moment.

—Douglas McKelvey & Hannah Hubin

Prayer Journal

AN ENTRY FOR

Cultivating an Awareness of God's Presence

FROM "A LITURGY FOR THE WRITING OF LITURGIES"

LORD, YOU HAVE SEARCHED ME AND KNOWN ME. YOU KNOW WHEN I SIT DOWN AND WHEN I STAND UP; YOU UNDERSTAND MY THOUGHTS FROM FAR AWAY. YOU OBSERVE MY TRAVELS AND MY REST; YOU ARE AWARE OF ALL MY WAYS. BEFORE A WORD IS ON MY TONGUE, YOU KNOW ALL ABOUT IT, LORD.
—PSALM 139: 1–4

POETRY READING: PSALM 139
PROSE READING: EXODUS 33:12–17

Inspire me to tell in words, of the holiness of
your presence made manifest in all tasks,
at all hours of all days.
  For you, O Lord, are with us always.

Every sphere of life and creation is Yours,
and all are threads of the same bright weave:
  our goings-out and our comings-in,
  our fellowship and our loneliness,
  our youth and our old age,
  our passions and our vocations,
  our chores and our entertainments.

You are equally present in our failures and
in our successes,
  in our sleep and in our wakeful hours,
  in our tears and in our laughter,
  in our births, in our lives,
and even in the hours of our deaths.
You are everpresent with us.

You are here. You are with me every moment.
Every moment is holy.

Amen.

DATE:

LOCATION:

- Consider a season or event in your life in which you easily caught sight of the Lord's presence. What do you think made the holiness of that moment so visible to you?

- Now consider a season or event in your life in which you struggled—or are struggling now—to see the Lord's presence. What do you think might be hiding the holiness of that moment from you?

- How does Moses's desire for the presence of the Lord relate to your own? How might David's recognition of the presence of the Lord challenge you to recognize every moment as holy?

RESPONSIVE PRAYER:

AN ENTRY ON

Renewal Amidst Discouragement

FROM "THE LITURGY OF THE HOURS: DAYBREAK"

POETRY READING: PSALM 32
PROSE READING: LUKE 5:27–32

I am weak and inconsistent,
and often buffeted by fear and pride
and selfishness. But being impoverished
and ill-equipped as I am,
I will look to the grace of God
and to the sanctifying work of the Spirit
to accomplish his purposes
in and through me this day,
as I, in grateful response,
seek to choose that which pleases him.

I open my heart anew to you,
O Lord, that the love of the Father
    and the life of Christ
    and the breath of the Spirit
would quicken within me
a greater affection for your ways.

Work your will in me.
Lead me this day, Lord Christ,
that I might walk its paths
in the light of the hope of my
coming redemption.

Amen.

JESUS REPLIED TO THEM, "IT IS NOT THOSE WHO ARE HEALTHY WHO NEED A DOCTOR, BUT THOSE WHO ARE SICK. I HAVE NOT COME TO CALL THE RIGHTEOUS, BUT SINNERS TO REPENTANCE."
—LUKE 5:31–32

DATE:

LOCATION:

- What weaknesses and inconsistencies burden you in this moment? How do your faults lead you to feel ill-equipped for the tasks ahead of you?

- How does the life and work of Christ comfort and lead you today? Consider the love of the Father and the presence of the Spirit within you as well. Yours is the forgiveness of a Trinitarian God. What joyful implications might this have for your present situation?

- Consider the truth that Christ came to call sinners, and that David calls himself blessed to be a forgiven sinner. How might your relationship with the Lord become more intimate through these acts of repentance and forgiveness?

RESPONSIVE PRAYER:

POETRY READING: PSALM 51
PROSE READING: 2 SAMUEL 11:1–12:25

Indeed, it was my desire to serve you well in this day, O God, but I have again fallen short of your righteousness in my thoughts, my intentions, my actions, and my utterances. I have responded at times without grace. I have chosen sometimes that which is unprofitable and which leads neither to my own flourishing nor to the proclamation of your glory. Forgive me, O King, for reasons both known and unknown. Forgive me for the harms I have done this day, and for the goods I might have done but failed to do; forgive me also for the constant condition of my heart, for the self-serving impulses, inclinations, and desires which stand me every moment in need of a savior.

How graciously you receive my repentances. May the grace of your forgiveness, which blooms evergreen for all your children, work powerfully in me, changing me into a better image-bearer of Christ and more faithful servant of my king.

Amen.

AN ENTRY ON

Repentance & Restoration

FROM "THE LITURGY OF THE HOURS: NIGHTFALL"

LET ME HEAR JOY
AND GLADNESS;
LET THE BONES YOU
HAVE CRUSHED REJOICE.
TURN YOUR FACE AWAY
FROM MY SINS AND
BLOT OUT ALL MY GUILT.
GOD, CREATE A
CLEAN HEART FOR ME
AND RENEW A STEADFAST
SPIRIT WITHIN ME.
—PSALM 51: 8–10

DATE:

LOCATION:

- Consider those things—done or left undone—over which you feel convicted today. What self-serving impulses might have given rise to these transgressions? Allow time for your words to bring shape to your repentance.

- Consider the grace of the Lord in receiving your repentance. Do not pass lightly over his mercy, but take time to write of his forgiveness and how his kindness shapes your own.

- Reflect on the story of David's sin and his own "journaling" of repentance and forgiveness. What might you add to the entries above after reading his?

RESPONSIVE PRAYER:

AN ENTRY ON

Having Believed a Lie

FROM "THE LITURGY OF THE HOURS: MIDDAY"

THEN JESUS SAID TO THE JEWS WHO HAD BELIEVED HIM, "IF YOU CONTINUE IN MY WORD, YOU REALLY ARE MY DISCIPLES. YOU WILL KNOW THE TRUTH, AND THE TRUTH WILL SET YOU FREE."
—JOHN 8:31–32

POETRY: PSALM 43
PROSE: JOHN 8:31–47

My heart has been tempted this day
to believe something about myself or others
that does not take into account your creation,
your mercy, your sacrifice, your grace,
your forgiveness, your redemption,
and your unshakeable love, O God.
Remind me again of these truths,
giving me faith enough to believe
and hope enough to choose
to embrace them again and again.

I have been swayed from the place of
resting in your grace today—swayed by shame,
by error, by vanity, by pride, or by love of the
praise of people. Act, O Holy Spirit!
Reveal my error, convict conscience,
and bring me to quick repentance.
Rekindle my affections, restoring them again
to their one worthy object, who is Christ,
and who alone holds the words of eternal life.

Shape my thoughts, O Lord, by your truth,
even as you shape my heart by your love.

Amen.

- What lies have taken root in your life (or in the lives of those you love) at this moment? What truths of God or his creation are you failing to take into account in believing these lies?

- What might it look like to have faith enough to believe and hope enough to choose the truths over the lies? Be specific in your reflection.

- Consider the freedom that comes with truth and the slavery that comes with believing these lies. How might living free indeed shape your heart and the pattern of your days, as you put aside all falsehood?

RESPONSIVE PRAYER:

AN ENTRY ON

Rest in the Midst of World-Weariness

FROM "A LITURGY FOR THOSE FLOODED BY TOO MUCH INFORMATION"

POETRY READING: PSALM 63
PROSE READING: MATTHEW 11:25–30

I am daily aware of more grief, O Lord,
than I can rightly consider,
of more suffering and scandal
than I can respond to, of more
hostility, hatred, horror, and injustice
than I can engage with compassion.

But you, O Jesus, are not disquieted
by such news of cruelty and terror and war.
You are neither anxious nor overwhelmed.
You carried the full weight of the suffering
of a broken world when you hung upon
the cross, and you carry it still.

When the cacophony of universal distress
unsettles us, remind us that we are but small
and finite creatures, never designed to carry
the vast abstractions of great burdens,
for our arms are too short and our strength
is too small. Justice and mercy, healing and
redemption, are your great labors.

Move each of us, liberated and empowered by
your Spirit, to fulfill the small part
of your redemptive work assigned to us.

Amen.

"COME TO ME, ALL OF YOU WHO ARE WEARY AND BURDENED, AND I WILL GIVE YOU REST. TAKE UP MY YOKE AND LEARN FROM ME, BECAUSE I AM LOWLY AND HUMBLE IN HEART, AND YOU WILL FIND REST FOR YOUR SOULS. FOR MY YOKE IS EASY AND MY BURDEN IS LIGHT."
—MATTHEW 11:28–30

- Take time to list those griefs wearying you in this moment. Lift each one to the Lord in prayer as honestly and specifically as you can.

- Now consider what part of God's redemptive work you might fulfill in these things. Again, be specific. Pray for Christ to guide your discernment as you weigh your role and strengthen your hands for the tasks ahead.

- Consider the reading from Matthew. How does the revelation to children and the relationship between the Father and the Son lead to an easy and light burden for those who choose Christ's yoke? How might this passage help you grow more receptive to true rest?

RESPONSIVE PRAYER:

AN ENTRY ON

Desire for Discernment

FROM "A LITURGY BEFORE CONSUMING MEDIA"

POETRY READING: PSALM 25:4–5
PROSE READING: ROMANS 14

O Discerning Spirit,
who alone judges all things rightly,
now be present in my mind and active
in my imagination as I prepare to engage
with the claims and questions of diverse cultures
incarnated in the stories that people tell.

Shape my vision by your fixed precepts,
and tutor me, Holy Spirit, that I might learn
to discern the difference between those stories
that are whole and those that are bent or broken.

Guard my mind against the old enticement
to believe a lie simply because it is beautifully
told. Let me not be careless. Give me right
conviction to judge my own motives in that
which I approve, teaching me to be always
mindful of that which I consume, and
thoughtful of the ways in which I consume it.
Impart to me keener knowledge of the limits
of my own heart in light of my own particular
brokenness, that I might choose what would
be for my flourishing and not for my harm.

Amen.

MAKE YOUR WAYS KNOWN TO ME, LORD; TEACH ME YOUR PATHS. GUIDE ME IN YOUR TRUTH AND TEACH ME, FOR YOU ARE THE GOD OF MY SALVATION; I WAIT FOR YOU ALL DAY LONG.
—PSALM 25:4–5

- What beautifully-told stories are enticing you towards lies at this moment? What is beautiful about them and what is deceptive? Clarify this distinction.What about these lies show a bent or broken truth?

- What does discernment look like for you, in your own life? What specific tendencies or temptations towards broken stories must you fight in your own heart? What might safeguarding your heart against these lies look like?

- What does discernment look like for you as you live in community with others? How might you, in love, help keep others from stumbling—acting not out of legalism, but out of grace?

RESPONSIVE PRAYER:

AN ENTRY ON

Help in Time of Temptation

FROM "A LITURGY FOR ONE BATTLING A DESTRUCTIVE DESIRE"

POETRY READING: PSALM 141
PROSE READING: JAMES 1:12–15

Jesus, here I am again,
desiring a thing
that were I to indulge in it
would war against my own heart,
and the hearts of those I love.

O Christ, rather let my life be thine!
Take my desires. Let them be subsumed
in still greater desire for you, until there remains
no room for these lesser cravings.

In this moment I might choose
to indulge a fleeting hunger,
or I might choose to love you more.

Faced with this temptation,
I would rather choose you, Jesus—
but I am weak. So be my strength.
I am shadowed. Be my light.
I am selfish. Unmake me now,
and refashion my desires
according to the better designs of your love.

Given the choice of shame or glory,
let me choose glory.
Given the choice of this moment or eternity,
let me choose in this moment what is eternal.

Amen.

BLESSED IS THE ONE WHO ENDURES TRIALS, BECAUSE WHEN HE HAS STOOD THE TEST HE WILL RECEIVE THE CROWN OF LIFE THAT GOD HAS PROMISED TO THOSE WHO LOVE HIM. NO ONE UNDERGOING A TRIAL SHOULD SAY, "I AM BEING TEMPTED BY GOD," SINCE GOD IS NOT TEMPTED BY EVIL, AND HE HIMSELF DOESN'T TEMPT ANYONE. BUT EACH PERSON IS TEMPTED WHEN HE IS DRAWN AWAY AND ENTICED BY HIS OWN EVIL DESIRE. THEN AFTER DESIRE HAS CONCEIVED, IT GIVES BIRTH TO SIN, AND WHEN SIN IS FULLY GROWN, IT GIVES BIRTH TO DEATH.

—JAMES 1:12–15

- Describe the destructive desire you are fighting. Try to identify the lesser cravings at the root of it. Can you identify any patterns in your life that might increase the severity of this war against your heart?

- Consider practical ways to fight for what is eternal even now in your daily choices. List scriptures, habits, prayers, forms of art, people in your life, etc. who may serve as your allies in this fight.

- Consider James' encouragement. Just as temptation leads ultimately to death, in what ways does fighting this temptation lead to a more abundant life?

RESPONSIVE PRAYER:

AN ENTRY ON

Meeting Christ in Seasons of Doubt

FROM "A LITURGY FOR NIGHTS & DAYS OF DOUBT"

SIMON PETER ANSWERED, "LORD, TO WHOM WILL WE GO? YOU HAVE THE WORDS OF ETERNAL LIFE. WE HAVE COME TO BELIEVE AND KNOW THAT YOU ARE THE HOLY ONE OF GOD.
— JOHN 6:68–69

POETRY READING: PSALM 22
PROSE READING: JOHN 6:22–69

I would that my heart was ever strong, O Lord,
my faith always firm and unwavering,
my thoughts unclouded,
my devotion sincere,
my vision clear.

But it is not always so.
There are those other moments,
as now,

when I cannot sense you near,
cannot hear you, see you, touch you—times
when fear or depression or frustration
overwhelm,
and I find no help or consolation,
when the seawalls of my faith crumble
and give way to inrushing tides of doubt.

And so, Jesus, I do now the only thing
I know to do.
Here I drag my heavy heart again
into this cleared and desolate space,
to see if you will meet me in my place of doubt.

For where else but to you might I flee
with my doubts? You alone have the
words of eternal life.

Amen.

- Here in this place of doubt and raw emotion, what questions do you have for your Lord? What would you ask of Christ, in confidence that he is listening? What do you have to say? Be honest about your pain and confusion. What emotions do you need to give expression to, in order to heave the weight of your doubt over to the hands of your God?

- Consider times in your life when your heart felt strong and your vision clear. Consider also other times of doubt, mapping out the seasons of your soul. Is there any pattern to the changes and variations? Listen to your life and the shape it has taken. Pay attention to where you are and where you have come from.

- Can you say honestly with Peter that there is no one else to whom you can go apart from Jesus? Why or why not? What does this say of your heart?

RESPONSIVE PRAYER:

POETRY READING: PSALM 103
PROSE READING: ROMANS 8:18–28

I sense your beckoning, O Lord,
and I willingly respond,
entering your presence
to plead on behalf of another.

Tune my thoughts,
  my words,
  my empathies
to articulate your greater heart,
your deeper purposes. I yield to your
intentions even unto the breaking of my
own heart for that which breaks yours.

Let this burden remain or return as often
as you would have me carry it again to you.

You are ever at work in this world.
So let my compassion be always active,
and my heart sensitive to your movements,
your promptings, your revelations.

Call us, your children,
always to care for one another
in prayer and in action,
in our various times of need.

Amen.

AN ENTRY ON

Compassion

FROM "A LITURGY FOR THOSE WITH A SUDDEN BURDEN TO INTERCEDE"

AS A FATHER HAS COMPASSION ON HIS CHILDREN, SO THE LORD HAS COMPASSION ON THOSE WHO FEAR HIM. FOR HE KNOWS WHAT WE ARE MADE OF, REMEMBERING THAT WE ARE DUST.
—PSALM 103:13–14

- Before considering your own place in the narrative of this situation, spend time considering the person you are seeking to love in this moment: their unique story, their individual wounds and desires. Try to remove yourself from the scene and focus entirely on the other. What are their greatest needs in this season?

- Now consider your own heart in this story. What role might you play? How do you see the Lord at work in your own life in ways that might benefit another?

- Consider the compassion of the Lord. Reflect on ways in which your compassion falls short of God's—places where your own desire to bring deliverance detracts from the true Deliverer. Pray that you might keep in step with the Spirit as you imitate the Father's compassion for this individual. In what specific ways might the compassion of Christ be manifest through you?

RESPONSIVE PRAYER:

AN ENTRY ON

Generosity

FROM "A LITURGY BEFORE GIVING I"

POETRY READING: PROVERBS 19:17
PROSE READING: 2 CORINTHIANS 9

In truth, I have nothing but you, O Christ,
nothing that I might call my own.

So let that good confession now
compel a better stewardship.

First teach me to treasure
you, Jesus, above all things. Then
let that increasing devotion be
increasingly demonstrated in a joyful
generosity—for to give is to live out
the declaration that you alone
are my provision and supply. I need
not fear what comes tomorrow.

Let me make each offering without
thought of temporal gain. Let me give
precisely because I have believed
your promises are true—and let
my giving be the proof.

Why should I grasp at that which I cannot
keep? This body will sleep in death and what
I now hold so briefly will pass into the keeping
of another. I own nothing here. I have no claim.
Dispel the myth of my possessions, lest they
taint that better hope of Heaven.

Amen.

NOW THE ONE WHO PROVIDES SEED FOR THE SOWER AND BREAD FOR FOOD WILL ALSO PROVIDE AND MULTIPLY YOUR SEED AND INCREASE THE HARVEST OF YOUR RIGHTEOUSNESS. YOU WILL BE ENRICHED IN EVERY WAY FOR ALL GENEROSITY, WHICH PRODUCES THANKSGIVING TO GOD THROUGH US.
—2 CORINTHIANS 9:10–11

- Consider any present struggles you have with generosity. What insecurities or doubts about God's promises do you have, that might lead to these struggles? What truths might you now preach to your own heart to replace those doubts?

- Reflect on ways the Lord has sustained or encouraged you in your own past acts of generosity. How has God already shown you that nothing is wasted when given to the Kingdom?

- Consider the generosity Christ demonstrated on earth. Reflect on ways small and large that you might more generously serve others.

RESPONSIVE PRAYER:

AN ENTRY ON

Comfort in Loneliness

FROM "A LITURGY BEFORE A MEAL EATEN ALONE"

POETRY READING: PSALM 27
PROSE READING: DEUTERONOMY 31:1–8

You created us for companionship,
O God, for the sharing of burdens,
for the joining of celebrations,
for the breaking of bread in fellowship,
and so it is not unnatural
that we should taste a particular sorrow
when passing our hours alone.

Sit with me and linger
in this solitary place, O Lord

In the absence of human companions,
may I know more fully your presence.
In this silence where there is no conversation,
may I more clearly hear your voice.

Use my own momentary loneliness
to work in me a more effectual sympathy
for others who are often alone,
and who long for the companionship
of their God and of his people.

Let me afterward be more intentional
in the practice of hospitality.
Let me sometimes be the reason
the loneliness of another is relieved.
Meet me now in my own loneliness, O Lord.

Amen.

LORD, HEAR MY VOICE WHEN I CALL; BE GRACIOUS TO ME AND ANSWER ME. MY HEART SAYS THIS ABOUT YOU:
"SEEK HIS FACE."
LORD, I WILL SEEK YOUR FACE.
DO NOT HIDE YOUR FACE FROM ME; DO NOT TURN YOUR SERVANT AWAY IN ANGER. YOU HAVE BEEN MY HELPER; DO NOT LEAVE ME OR ABANDON ME,
GOD OF MY SALVATION.
—PSALM 27:7–9

- How might you use the presence of people, activities, and noise in your life as a means to avoid difficult thoughts, emotions, and fears? Take time to reflect on those things that might rise to the surface of your heart in this time alone, with the peace of knowing that the Lord is present with you as you process.

- Consider ways others in your life have relieved your loneliness at certain points. In what ways—through what actions or words—did they make their presence gently known to you? Who in your life might be lonely in this season, and how might you relieve their loneliness in similar ways?

- Consider what it means to seek the face of the Lord in times like these. How might you make this a regular habit, even when you are not alone?

RESPONSIVE PRAYER:

AN ENTRY ON

Competition

FROM "A LITURGY FOR THOSE WHO COMPETE"

SO LET THE ONE WHO BOASTS, BOAST IN THE LORD. FOR IT IS NOT THE ONE COMMENDING HIMSELF WHO IS APPROVED, BUT THE ONE THE LORD COMMENDS.
—2 CORINTHIANS 10:17–18

POETRY READING: PROVERBS 27:17
PROSE READING: 2 CORINTHIANS 10

There are, O Lord, eternal patterns—
fragments of the story of redemption—
etched into our competitions—
each small echoes
of the fights that a life of long obedience
to Christ might entail.

Teach me to be
gracious in victory,
and gracious in defeat,
remembering that in this competitive context
I am first your emissary,
a representative of your
emerging redemption extended
even onto the fields of competition.

Let me never love winning more
than I love those against whom I compete.

Let me model what it is to be
one fiercely focused on, and invested in,
the drama at hand,
pushing myself always towards the goal,
and yet ever extending
a humility and graciousness
in keeping with my status
as your servant, O Christ.

Amen.

- Consider the ways you might be sharpened in this competitive experience. Pause from thinking about those you compete against and reflect instead on the ways you might personally seek to improve through this task—physically, mentally, emotionally, spiritually. If the only one present with you now was the Lord, what would your goal be?

- Now consider your fellow competitors and the whole of their lives—physical, mental, emotional, and spiritual. How might you love, care for, and encourage them even in the midst of this competition?

- Consider the goal before you. What might it mean for you to boast in the Lord in this?

RESPONSIVE PRAYER:

AN ENTRY ON

Missing Someone

FROM "A LITURGY FOR MISSING SOMEONE"

POETRY READING: PROVERBS 17:17
PROSE READING: JOHN 16:16–22

You created our hearts for unbroken fellowship.
Yet the constraints of time and place, and the
stuttering rhythms of life in a fallen world
dictate that all fellowships in these days
will at times be broken or incomplete.

I acknowledge, O Lord, that it is
a right and a good thing to miss deeply
those whom I love but with whom
I cannot be physically present.
Grant me, therefore, courage to love well
even in this time of absence.

I praise you, knowing that these glad
aches are a true measure of the bonds
you have wrought between our hearts.

Use even this sadness to carve out spaces
in my soul where still greater repositories of
holy affection might be held, unto the end that
we might better love, in times of absence and in
times of presence alike.

How I look forward, O Lord, to the day
when all our fellowships will be restored,
eternal and unbroken.

Amen.

SO YOU ALSO HAVE SORROW NOW. BUT I WILL SEE YOU AGAIN. YOUR HEARTS WILL REJOICE, AND NO ONE WILL TAKE AWAY YOUR JOY FROM YOU.
—JOHN 16:22

- Reflect in gratitude on the person you miss in this moment. In what ways do you see God in them? Thank the Lord for the unique ways he has revealed himself to you through this divine image-bearer.

- Reflect also on memories and seasons the two of you have shared together. How have you walked alongside one another? Thank the Lord also for granting you these moments in which you were not alone.

- Consider ways in which you might love or honor this person, even when you are not physically present with them. Look specifically for ways that acknowledge and celebrate your unique relationship with them and the unique space that exists between the two of you that no one else shares.

RESPONSIVE PRAYER:

AN ENTRY ON

Homesickness

FROM "A LITURGY FOR AN INCONSOLABLE HOMESICKNESS"

POETRY READING: PSALM 84
PROSE READING: ECCLESIASTES 3:11

It is a good, good thing to have a home.

But now that I have gone from it, let me steward
well, O God, this homesick gift, as I know my
wish for what has been is not some solitary
ache but is woven with a deeper longing
for what will one day be.

This yearning to return to what I knew is,
even more than that, a yearning for a place
my eyes have yet to see.

HE HAS MADE EVERYTHING APPROPRIATE IN ITS TIME. HE HAS ALSO PUT ETERNITY IN THEIR HEARTS, BUT NO ONE CAN DISCOVER THE WORK GOD HAS DONE FROM BEGINNING TO END.
—ECCLESIASTES 3:11

So let me steward this sacred yearning well.
Homesickness is indeed a holy thing,
like the slow burning of an immortal beacon,
set ablaze to bid us onward.

The shape of that ache for another time
and place is the imprint of eternity
within our souls.

So let those sorrows do their work in me,
O God. Let them stir such yearnings as would
fix my journey forward towards that place for
which I've always pined.

Amen.

- Consider what interactions, encounters, or memories have led you to this current sense of homesickness. What has brought about this longing? Whether in joy or lament, entrust those memories to the Lord's keeping.

- Consider the various homes you have known—the different places you might sometimes pine for. What elements of those homes seem to echo, in a limited and temporal way, the eternal longings in your soul? In what specific ways do these homes anticipate the dwelling place of the Lord?

- Consider the pilgrimage you are taking, much like the Psalmist, going from strength to strength and home to home. In what ways might this moment of homesickness serve as renewal for the journey?

RESPONSIVE PRAYER:

AN ENTRY ON

Fearing Failure

FROM "A LITURGY FOR THOSE FEARING FAILURE"

I AM SURE OF THIS, THAT HE WHO STARTED A GOOD WORK IN YOU WILL CARRY IT ON TO COMPLETION UNTIL THE DAY OF CHRIST JESUS.
—PHILIPPIANS 1:6

POETRY READING: PSALM 37
PROSE READING: PHILIPPIANS 1:3–11

I come to you, O Christ,
in dismay, fearing I might fail
in what is now before me.

Let my fears of failure drive me,
O Lord, to collapse here upon your
strong shoulders, and here to rest,
reminded again that I and all of your
children are always utterly dependent upon
you to bring to completion, in and through
us, the good works which you have prepared
beforehand for us to do. It is not my own
work that is before me now, but yours!

I have but one task:
to be faithful.

The success of my endeavors is not mine to
judge. You work in ways that I cannot comprehend.
And in your economy, there will be no waste.
Even what I have judged as failure,
You will tool to greater purpose.

Use then, O Lord, even my failures, and my
fears of failing, to advance your purposes in
my heart and in your kingdom and in this
world. My confidence is only in you.

Amen.

- Consider the fears you are facing. What are the ways in which you believe you might fail? What insecurities or doubts are at work in your heart for each one? Seek to hand each fear, with its accompanying doubts, to your Lord.

- Reflect on times in your life when you have failed by your own standards. How did you see the Lord over time bringing fruitfulness even from what you had judged as failure? In what ways are you still waiting on him to redeem those old moments of fear?

- What might your one task—to be faithful—look like right now? In what specific ways is the Lord inviting you to invest in his economy of grace, mercy, and redemption?

RESPONSIVE PRAYER:

AN ENTRY ON

Trusting God Amidst the Death of a Dream

FROM "A LITURGY FOR THE DEATH OF A DREAM"

POETRY READING: PROVERBS 3:3–12
PROSE READING: EPHESIANS 2

O Christ, in whom the final fulfillment
of all hope is held secure,
I bring to you now the weathered
fragments of my former dreams.
What I so wanted
has not come to pass.

My disappointments
reveal so much about my own agenda
for my life, and the ways I quietly demand
that it should play out: free of conflict,
free of pain, free of want.

My dreams are all so small.
So let this disappointment do its work.

You are the King of my collapse.
You answer not what I demand,
but what I do not even know to ask.

Now take this dream, this husk,
this chaff of my desire, and give it back
reformed and remade according to
your better vison,
or do not give it back at all.

Not my dreams, O Lord,
not my dreams,
but yours, be done.

Amen.

FOR WE ARE HIS WORKMANSHIP, CREATED IN CHRIST JESUS FOR GOOD WORKS, WHICH GOD PREPARED AHEAD OF TIME FOR US TO DO.
—EPHESIANS 2:10

- Consider the dream that has recently crumbled. How much weight have you asked it to bear in your life? How much hope and security have you entrusted to this dream?

- What does it mean for your Lord to be the "King of your collapse?" How does this shape the way you lament the death of this dream?

- Like the authors of the Proverbs passage and the apostle's letter, how might you look to the promises and preparations of God as you pray for a remade dream? How might these passages even now mold your heart to desire greater things?

RESPONSIVE PRAYER:

AN ENTRY ON

Restoration After Doing Harm

FROM "A LITURGY FOR THOSE WHO HAVE DONE HARM"

POETRY READING: PSALM 25:6–22
PROSE READING: JAMES 5:13–18

I have harmed another, O Lord, and now
I have neither peace nor rest.

Forgive me, most merciful Father,
for by sinning against one that you have placed
in my life for me to love and be merciful toward,
I have sinned against you.
I confess, O God, that I have broken faith,
broken trust, wounded another,
and for this I repent.

For the sake of the one I have offended,
O Lord, grant them the grace
of true forgiveness and the freedom
that would follow from it.
Let them rise to continue their journey
toward you unhindered.
And let me rise from this conviction
and confession wiser in my faith,
more intentional in my love for others,
less likely to choose the dried husk of selfishness
when next tempted toward sin.

Forgive me, O Lord, lest I despair.
Restore me, lest I be forever lost.
Embrace me again to life
and to right standing with you, O God,
and to the fellowship of love
and compassion that is your church.

Amen.

THEREFORE, CONFESS YOUR SINS TO ONE ANOTHER AND PRAY FOR ONE ANOTHER, SO THAT YOU MAY BE HEALED. THE PRAYER OF A RIGHTEOUS PERSON IS VERY POWERFUL IN ITS EFFECT.
—JAMES 5:16

- Consider times when you have been forgiven before—by people in your family, by your community, and by the Lord. Remember that path towards restoration, the kindness extended to you, and ways in which you have already seen the Lord bring good out of the hurt you caused. How does this inform your hope now?

- Consider times when you have forgiven another who has wronged you. How might your own journey of forgiveness inform your patience and kindness towards those now called to forgive you?

- Consider the words of James on the significance of prayer for both physical and spiritual healing. Reflect on ways you can continue to make prayer a regular part of this journey of reconciliation for you.

RESPONSIVE PRAYER:

AN ENTRY FOR

Seasons of Sorrow

FROM "A LITURGY FOR THOSE WHO WEEP WITHOUT KNOWNING WHY"

WHEN JESUS SAW HER CRYING, AND THE JEWS WHO HAD COME WITH HER CRYING, HE WAS DEEPLY MOVED IN HIS SPIRIT AND TROUBLED. "WHERE HAVE YOU PUT HIM?" HE ASKED. "LORD," THEY TOLD HIM, "COME AND SEE." JESUS WEPT. SO THE JEWS SAID, "SEE HOW HE LOVED HIM!"
— JOHN 11:33–36

POETRY READING: PSALM 130
PROSE READING: JOHN 11:1–44

O Lord, how can we not weep,
when waking each day in this vale of tears?
How can we not feel those pangs,
when we, wounded by others,
so soon learn to wound as well,
and in the end wound even ourselves?
We grieve what we cannot heal and
we grieve our half-belief,
having made uneasy peace
with disillusion, aligning ourselves with a
self-protective lie that would have us kill our
best hopes just to keep our disappointments
half-confined.

And yet, there is somewhere in our tears,
a hope still kept.

Jesus also wept.
You wept.

And the grief of God is no small thing,
and the weeping of God is not without effect.
The tears of Jesus preceded
a resurrection of the dead.

Oh Spirit of God,
is it then possible
that our tears might also be
a kind of intercession?

Amen.

- Reflect on this moment of sorrow for you—the occasion, the cause, and the places you have already sought comfort and found it lacking. Do you feel alone in this sorrow? How might remembering the tears of Christ shape this moment for you?

- Reflect on the last few times you have witnessed someone else weeping—the occasion, the cause, your presence there. How might remembering the tears of Christ shape your compassion towards another's tears?

- The liturgy excerpt here ends with a question. Continue the next few lines, explaining and expounding on this question to the Lord in your own words.

RESPONSIVE PRAYER:

AN ENTRY FOR

Difficult Anniversaries

FROM "A LITURGY FOR THE ANNIVERSARY OF A LOSS"

THEN THE ONE SEATED ON THE THRONE SAID, "LOOK, I AM MAKING EVERYTHING NEW." HE ALSO SAID, "WRITE, BECAUSE THESE WORDS ARE FAITHFUL AND TRUE."
—REVELATION 21:5

POETRY READING: ISAIAH 55:6–13
PROSE READING: REVELATION 21:1–5

I have felt its approach in the
back of my mind, O Lord,
like a burden tilting
toward me across the calendar.
I have felt its long approach,
and now it has arrived.

This is the day that marks
the anniversary of my loss,
and waking to it, I must
drink again from
the stream of sorrow.

O Christ, redeem this day.

I do not ask that these lingerings
of grief be erased, but that
the fingers of your grace
would work this memory
into a form holding now in
that same sorrow the surety
of your presence, so that
when I look again at that loss,
I see you in the deepest gloom
of it, weeping with me,
even as I hear you whispering
that this is not the end, but only the still,
grey of a dawn before the world begins.

Amen.

- Consider the grief you continue to carry today, though the initial shock of loss might have softened. What has it meant for these griefs to exist in the space of your relationship with the Lord?

- Consider the struggles that you have been able, at least in part, to lay to rest since the initial loss. What things do you no longer carry with you each day? What has helped you lay them down?

- Just as this day serves as a memorial of something past, it also serves as a signpost of a greater day to come, when everything lost is restored. Reflect on this anniversary, not merely as a revisiting of grief, but as a complicated middle between tragedy and triumph.

RESPONSIVE PRAYER:

AN ENTRY ON

the Loss of Possessions

FROM "A LITURGY FOR THOSE WHO SUFFER LOSS FROM FIRE, FLOOD, OR STORM"

POETRY READING: ISAIAH 40:1–11
PROSE READING: MATTHEW 6:19–34

O Christ in Whom
our Treasures are Secure,
fix now our hope in you.

In light of all that was so suddenly lost,
O Lord, in light of all we had gathered
but could not keep,
comfort us.

Let us not lose sight of the truth
that we live in the midst of an
unfolding story of redemption, and that
even this loss of ours will have its
counterpoint
at the great restoration.

Let us see that
even in disaster, there is grace still
at work, for you know the limits
of our hearts.

"THE GRASS WITHERS, THE FLOWERS FADE, BUT THE WORD OF OUR GOD REMAINS FOREVER."
—ISAIAH 40:8

Be with us now as we slog merely to reclaim
some fraction of that which we
once took for granted.

Let our rebuilding be a
declaration that a day will come when
all good things are permanent.

Amen.

- Consider the material things you have lost. How much weight have you asked them to bear in your life? How much hope and security have you entrusted to them? Spend time reflecting as well on any immaterial things in your life that seem lost along with these possessions, such as a sense of peace or well-being.

- Consider the labor ahead of you as you seek to reclaim or rebuild what you have lost. How might you build again more faithfully than you did the first time? How might you more fully entrust these things to the Lord, acknowledging that all you have is God's?

- Reflect on the endurance of the Word of God in a world filled with temporary things. How might this loss lead you to a greater affection for the Word of the Lord? How does the psalmist's image of God as our rock become a more tangible and experienced reality in the midst of this hard season?

RESPONSIVE PRAYER:

POETRY READING: ISAIAH 43:16–21
PROSE READING: JOHN 10:11–18

AN ENTRY ON

Beginning Something New

FROM "A LITURGY FOR FIRST WAKING"

I am not the captain of my own destiny,
nor even of this new work, and so
I renounce again all claim
to my own life and desires.
I am only yours, O Lord.
Lead me by your mercies through this season,
that I might spend my hours well,
not in harried pursuit of my own agendas,
but rather in good service to you.

Teach me to shepherd these small duties
with great love,
tending faithfully to those tasks
you place within my care
and tending with patience and
kindness the needs and hearts of
those people you place within my reach.

Nothing is too hard for you, Lord Christ.
I deposit now all confidence in you
that whatever this journey brings,
my foundations will not be shaken.

In all things your grace will sustain me.
Bid me follow, and I will follow.

Amen.

"DO NOT REMEMBER
THE PAST EVENTS;
PAY NO ATTENTION TO
THINGS OF OLD.
LOOK, I AM ABOUT TO DO
SOMETHING NEW;
EVEN NOW IT IS COMING.
DO YOU NOT SEE IT?
INDEED, I WILL MAKE A WAY IN
THE WILDERNESS,
RIVERS IN THE DESERT."
—ISAIAH 43:18–19

- What might it look like for you to renounce your claim to this new work, recognizing that much of it is out of your control? Are there any parts of this new endeavor you feel you are trying to accomplish purely by your own strength and will? If so, why?

- Consider the new works of the Lord. What does it look like for the Lord to begin a new thing, and how might you embrace the renewing work of God in this new task?

- Consider the image of Christ as shepherd as you seek to shepherd these small duties before you. How might you follow in the footsteps of Jesus in this, imitating his gentle strength and his trust in the Father?

RESPONSIVE PRAYER:

AN ENTRY ON

Stewardship

FROM "A LITURGY FOR THOSE WITH AN IMPULSE TO BUY"

POETRY READING: PROVERBS 3:9–10
PROSE READING: MATTHEW 19:16–30

Let me learn to love you enough, O Lord,
that I need no constant stream of bright and
shiny things to ease some itch or ache within
my soul. Free my heart from craven clenching,
as if ownership of a thing could ever
bring about the gain of anything eternal.

I know I cannot keep the things I hold, and so
I would not sleepwalk through this life, always
amassing that which will be of no true benefit.

Let me instead, O Lord, tend well what you
have trusted to my keeping, planting good seed
for future reaping in eternal fields.

Let me learn by practice what it means to
seek first your kingdom,
your purposes,
your glory.

Amen.

HONOR THE LORD WITH
YOUR POSSESSIONS
AND WITH THE FIRST PRODUCE
OF YOUR ENTIRE HARVEST;
THEN YOUR BARNS WILL BE
COMPLETELY FILLED,
AND YOUR VATS WILL
OVERFLOW WITH NEW WINE.
—PROVERBS 3:9–10

- Reflect on the things you treasure and the things you desire. What might be lulling you to sleepwalk through life? What holy craving might you be attempting to fill with a lesser thing?

- Consider your field of vocation, and your relationships and responsibilities in family and community. What has the Lord entrusted to you to keep and tend and nurture?

- Consider Christ's call to forsake all else to follow him. How is the concept of stewardship key to the life of faith?

RESPONSIVE PRAYER:

AN ENTRY FOR

Reorienting the Heart in Times of Irritation

FROM "A LITURGY FOR A FLEETING IRRITATION"

DON'T WORRY ABOUT ANYTHING, BUT IN EVERYTHING, THROUGH PRAYER AND PETITION WITH THANKSGIVING, PRESENT YOUR REQUESTS TO GOD. AND THE PEACE OF GOD, WHICH SURPASSES ALL UNDERSTANDING, WILL GUARD YOUR HEARTS AND MINDS IN CHRIST JESUS.
—PHILIPPIANS 4:6–7

POETRY READING: PROVERBS 25:11–15
PROSE READING: PHILIPPIANS 4:4–9

I bring to you, Lord, my momentary irritation,
that you might reveal the buried seed of it—
not in the words or actions of another person,
but in the withered and hypocritical expectations
of my own small heart. Uproot from this
impoverished soil all arrogance and insecurity that
would prompt me to dismiss or disdain others,
judging them with a less generous measure than
I reckon when judging myself.

Prune away the tangled growth
of my own unjustified irritations, Jesus,
and graft to my heart instead your humility,
    your compassion,
    your patience,
    your kindness,

that I might bear good fruit in keeping
with your grace.

Amen.

- Consider the source of this current irritation—both the external cause and the tangled desires of your soul in response. In what ways might you better understand your own insecurities and woundedness in light of this irritated response? How might you bring this before the Lord?

- Consider the ways you have responded out of irritation in this situation—to another person, to the Lord, to your own heart. Is there repentance to be made?

- Reflect on the peace of God. What might it mean for the peace of God to guard your heart and mind in this moment of irritation and in irritations to come?

RESPONSIVE PRAYER:

AN ENTRY ON

Trusting During a Time of Fear

FROM "A LITURGY FOR ONE WHO HAS SUFFERED A NIGHTMARE"

POETRY READING: PSALM 23
PROSE READING: LUKE 12:22–34

I am afraid,
    in need of your comfort, O God.
I am in darkness,
    in need of your light.

    Father, keep watch.
    Spirit, calm fear.
    Jesus, be near.

Your presence abides
with your children forever,
and I am your child.
Therefore, I know that you are with me.

    I am not alone.
    I am never alone.
    You are here.

Kindle in my heart the fires of holy affection,
casting out all disturbing shadows.

Let me draw courage
from your fierce and unyielding love,
even in moments when I am afraid.

Amen.

EVEN WHEN I GO THROUGH
THE DARKEST VALLEY,
I FEAR NO DANGER,
FOR YOU ARE WITH ME;
YOUR ROD AND YOUR STAFF—
THEY COMFORT ME.
—PSALM 23:4

- Describe those things you fear as specifically as you feel you can. Being able to put something into words naturally gives it limitations. See the fears you carry, individualized and isolated, and offer them to the Lord.

- What is the significance of knowing God is present with you when you're fighting fear? How does the certainty of God's love foster courage in our souls?

- Reflect on scripture's use of sheep and shepherd imagery when discussing fear. What is the significance here? How might leaning into this image in your own moments of fear serve as a comfort?

RESPONSIVE PRAYER:

POETRY READING: PSALM 145
PROSE READING: JEREMIAH 29:13–14

I am stirred and saddened, O Lord,
to bid farewell and return now
from my sojourn in that place
where longings for something
more than the life I lead
were wakened.

Let this beauty do its work in me,
inviting me to dig beneath these
fresh-stirred longings, to see
that their roots are, in truth,
profound and holy wounds,
yearnings for a lost garden and a more
perfect city.

Thank you, O my God,
for loving me enough
that you would rouse
my deepest desires again.

May I return now
to the daily details of my own life
with truer vision and fiercer hope,
trailing with me
remnants of that coming glory
I have glimpsed again.

Amen.

AN ENTRY ON

Experiencing Beauty Created By Human Hands

FROM "A LAMENT UPON THE FINISHING OF A BELOVED BOOK"

YOU WILL CALL TO ME AND COME AND PRAY TO ME, AND I WILL LISTEN TO YOU. YOU WILL SEEK ME AND FIND ME WHEN YOU SEARCH FOR ME WITH ALL YOUR HEART.
—JEREMIAH 29:12–13

- Describe the longings this work has evoked. What details have left their impression upon you, and why? What hope feels nearer now to you than before you encountered this work?

- Describe the process of returning to "regular life" after encountering this work—coming down from the mountain and resuming your own labors again. Is it frustrating, disappointing, discouraging? Or is it encouraging and invigorating? How might you carry the hope you have found into your daily labors now?

- Jeremiah assures us that we will find the Lord when we seek him. Reflect on this truth in relation to the longings this work has evoked in you. How might the beauty that you have encountered in this work be beauty you can draw near to?

RESPONSIVE PRAYER:

AN ENTRY ON

Experiencing Beauty Created By God

FROM "A LITURGY FOR SUNSETS"

POETRY READING: PSALM 19
PROSE READING: GENESIS 1

You have infused your created order
with an inexplicable beauty
that is inseparable from
the expression of your nature.

Open my heart therefore
to the work of your beauty,
to the echoes of your glory
written upon this your creation.

May this meditation upon your glories
not leave me unmoved. May I receive the
expression of this beauty as I would the
lavish endearments of a love letter.

Tender my heart to receive it.

May the patterns of your eternal beauties
be fixed in my soul, O Lord,

that the life I lead and the words I speak
might hereafter be infused with a grace
that would show forth your beauty.

May your people be as winsome as this created beauty,
O God, and give as little cause for offense,
as they carry your name, your truth,
and your love into this world.

Amen.

IN THE BEGINNING GOD CREATED THE HEAVENS AND THE EARTH.
—GENESIS 1:1

- Describe the created beauty you have encountered. How is this beauty inseparable from the nature of God? In what way might you know your Lord better after this encounter?

- What would it mean for some pattern of God's eternal beauty to be more fixed in your soul after this encounter? What winsomeness here in nature might you seek to imitate?

- Reflect on the Psalmist's correlation between the beauty of nature and the Word of the Lord. How might you move from this encounter with nature to a similar gratitude for scripture and the Spirit?

RESPONSIVE PRAYER:

POETRY READING: HOSEA 6:1–3
PROSE READING: JAMES 4:16–17

May I recall the work which
you have done for your people,
O Christ, and the work which you are now
doing, in me. Stir by your Holy Spirit
my heart and memory and conscience.

Open my eyes to see my own faults,
my own weaknesses, the harms I have
caused and the griefs I have inflicted—
Not so that I would sit in an impassable guilt,
but so that I would be stirred
to fresh repentance, to the making of amends
where amends can be made, and to prayer
and trust that your Spirit might cleanse
those things which I have stained by my own
selfishness, bitterness, jealousy, pride,
or impatience.

Remind me of the righteousness that is now mine,
of the ongoing forgiveness that you extend,
of your work on my behalf
which is both finished, and forever
ongoing and necessary in this life.

In Christ you have declared me righteous.
Yet by your Spirit I pray you would ever
continue to cleanse me, sanctifying me that
my aroma, day to day and week to week
might be more and more like that of Christ.

Amen.

AN ENTRY ON

Feeling a Sense of Conviction

FROM "A LITURGY FOR LAUNDERING"

COME, LET'S RETURN
TO THE LORD.
FOR HE HAS TORN US,
AND HE WILL HEAL US;
HE HAS WOUNDED US,
AND HE WILL BIND UP OUR
WOUNDS. HE WILL REVIVE US
AFTER TWO DAYS,
AND ON THE THIRD DAY HE
WILL RAISE US UP
SO WE CAN LIVE IN HIS
PRESENCE. LET'S STRIVE TO
KNOW THE LORD.
HIS APPEARANCE IS
AS SURE AS THE DAWN.
HE WILL COME TO US LIKE
THE RAIN, LIKE THE SPRING
SHOWERS THAT WATER
THE LAND.
—HOSEA 6:1–3

- Reflect on where you sense conviction, and pray for the Lord to open your eyes. Consider what you have done and what you have left undone, bringing both before Christ.

- Consider your hesitancy towards conviction. What means of self-protection do you utilize to avoid pressing on to know the Lord? What fears do you carry when you allow yourself to fall so open before God?

- Reflect on the righteousness that is already yours and the ongoing work of Christ in your life. What tensions do you sense between these two realities?

RESPONSIVE PRAYER:

AN ENTRY ON

Cultivating a Desire for God's Word

FROM "A LITURGY FOR MONDAY'S TABLE BLESSING"

POETRY READING: PSALM 119:1–24
PROSE READING: JOHN 14

O God my rock,
I thank you that you
did not leave us rudderless and
tossed by storms in this life,
but have graciously given us,
in your word, and in the witness of
the life and words of your son,
a true mooring for our lives,
a true anchor for our souls.

Your words are life to me,
Lord Christ.

Even as I might hunger for the tastes
and textures and aromas of
a meal spread before me,
I pray you would also daily increase
my deep hunger for your words
and your truth,
that my words
and choices
and actions
would be shaped
by your gracious revelation.

Amen.

"LORD," THOMAS SAID, "WE DON'T KNOW WHERE YOU'RE GOING. HOW CAN WE KNOW THE WAY? JESUS TOLD HIM, "I AM THE WAY, THE TRUTH, AND THE LIFE. NO ONE COMES TO THE FATHER EXCEPT THROUGH ME.
—JOHN 14:5–6

- What truths are you seeking and what questions are you asking in this season? What might it mean for the words of Christ to be life to you as you seek and ask?

- Consider truths you have relied on in the past when tossed by storms. What truths have remained crucial to you as you journey through life—truths without which you would not be where you are today?

- Reflect on the significance of the Word of God and the Spirit of God as we follow Christ to the Kingdom. How does Christ—as Truth himself—serve to lead us on?

RESPONSIVE PRAYER:

AN ENTRY ON

Praise for Small Things

FROM "A LITURGY FOR THURSDAY'S TABLE BLESSING"

POETRY READING: PSALM 104:14–15
PROSE READING: LUKE 2:1–7

O King of Joys Eternal,
today I praise you for small wonders;
in them I see your delight.

For birds that trill and warble their worship,
for the verdant witness of windblown leaves,
and of starlight sparkling, and of sunlit streams,
and of blooming flowers,

I praise you, O King.
Your joy is everywhere manifest,
even in the smallest things.

I praise you, O King,
for soft beds and blankets,
for stories and songs,
for kisses and kindnesses.
Your tenderness is displayed
in all things nurturing.

Your mercy in manifest in the details
of this world, O Lord.
Your grace is worked into
every corner of creation.
For all small wonders,
I give you thanks and I
give you praise, O God.

Amen.

HE CAUSES GRASS TO GROW
FOR THE LIVESTOCK
AND PROVIDES CROPS FOR
MAN TO CULTIVATE,
PRODUCING FOOD
FROM THE EARTH,
WINE THAT MAKES
HUMAN HEARTS GLAD—
MAKING HIS FACE SHINE
WITH OIL—AND BREAD
THAT SUSTAINS
HUMAN HEARTS.
—PSALM 104:14–15

- Take time to list small things that bring you delight, things for which you might honestly offer praise. Include works of God both tangible and intangible. Thinking through a normal day's schedule may aid in recalling small gifts so easily taken for granted.

- Consider now small moments in your life that have spoken to you of grace. Remember simple encounters, small words and phrases, short glimpses that have communicated the love of God to you.

- Consider the coming of Christ as a newborn. How does this true story of God making himself to be one of the smallest parts of his own creation speak to the Lord's glory manifest even in small things?

RESPONSIVE PRAYER:

AN ENTRY ON

Praise for Mighty Things

FROM "A LITURGY FOR FRIDAY'S TABLE BLESSING"

HE ESTABLISHED THE EARTH
ON ITS FOUNDATIONS;
IT WILL NEVER BE SHAKEN.
YOU COVERED IT
WITH THE DEEP
AS IF IT WERE A GARMENT;
THE WATER STOOD
ABOVE THE MOUNTAINS.
AT YOUR REBUKE
THE WATER FLED;
AT THE SOUND OF YOUR
THUNDER THEY
HURRIED AWAY—
MOUNTAINS ROSE
AND VALLEYS SANK—
TO THE PLACE YOU
ESTABLISHED FOR THEM.
YOU SET A BOUNDARY
THEY CANNOT CROSS;
THEY WILL NEVER COVER
THE EARTH AGAIN.
—PSALM 104:5–9

POETRY READING: PSALM 104:5–9
PROSE READING: EPHESIANS 1:15–23

O God of power and strength,
today I offer praise for things
larger and mightier than myself.
For these I give you thanks,
for they remind us that we are small beside
you, our Maker, and that we are the children
of a mighty God and Father.

I give you thanks for all things magnificent,
mighty, monumental, for great creatures
and colossal planets and all things that set us
in awe of what is vaster than ourselves.
These things render us good service, O Lord,
for the wonder they inspire is a window directing
our eyes and our thoughts to you, who are vaster
and more infinite and awesome, who are fiercer
in your love and mightier in your strength
and more holy in your righteousness
than all created things.

I, your child, am small before you,
but I am greatly loved.

And so I bow my head in thanks.

Amen.

- Take time to list mighty things to which you respond with awe, and which might rightly move you to praise of their Maker. Include works of God both tangible and intangible. Lean into the grandeur of thunderstorms and mountain peaks and the grandeur of mercy and love.

- Consider ways in which you have taken some of these mighty works for granted. In humility, acknowledge your need for yet another mighty work of God—the life of Christ in us—to begin to live in proper gratitude and praise.

- Reflect as a small child before a mighty God. What comfort do you take in the Lord's magnificence? What fears do you experience? What questions?

RESPONSIVE PRAYER:

POETRY READING: PSALM 102:1–7
PROSE READING: 2 CORINTHIANS 4:7–14

We were not made for mortality
but for immortality; our souls are
ever in their prime, and so the faltering of
our physical bodies repeatedly takes us by surprise.

Even so, may the inescapable decline
of our bodies here not be wasted.
May it do its tutoring work, inclining
our hearts and souls ever more vigorously
toward your coming kingdom, O God.

While we rightly pray for healing and relief,
and sometimes receive the respite of such
blessings, give us also patience for the enduring
of whatever hardships our journeys entail.

For what we endure here,
in the deterioration of bone and joint,
blood and marrow, muscle and ligament,
vitality and mobility and clarity,
is but our own small share of the malady
common to a frayed creation,
yet yearning for a promised restoration.

Give us humility therefore in our infirmities,
to ask and to receive, day by day,
your mercies as our needs require,
reminding us that this flesh and blood
are soon to be transformed, redeemed, remade.

Amen.

AN ENTRY ON

Experiencing a Season of Illness

FROM "A LITURGY FOR FOR THE FEELING OF INFIRMITIES"

THEREFORE WE DO NOT GIVE UP. EVEN THOUGH OUR OUTER PERSON IS BEING DESTROYED, OUR INNER PERSON IS BEING RENEWED DAY BY DAY.
—2 CORINTHIANS 4:16

- Consider this moment of pause that often comes with infirmity. What might this pause be inviting you into? Reflect on the unique opportunities that present themselves in this moment: humility to ask and receive, dependence on others, humor towards limitations that have already been conquered by Christ, hope in resurrection, etc.

- This liturgy is spoken in first person plural, for physical infirmity of one degree or another is shared by all those who live in a fallen world. How might this moment work in you a greater compassion for the suffering of others?

- The apostle reminds us that the feeling of infirmities contrasts with the daily renewal of our souls. How might you use this time of illness as a time of renewal—moving towards greater spiritual health and strength, even as your body remains weak?

RESPONSIVE PRAYER:

AN ENTRY ON

the Good Work of Waiting

FROM "A LITURGY FOR WAITING IN LINE"

POETRY READING: ECCLESIASTES 7:8–13
PROSE READING: JAMES 5:7–11

As my life is lived in anticipation
of the redemption of all things,
so let this time of waiting
be to my own heart
a living parable and a teaching moment.
Do not waste even my petty irritations, O Lord.
Use them to expose my sin and selfishness
and to reshape my vision
and my desire into better, holier things.

Decrease my unrighteous impatience,
directed at circumstances and people.
Increase instead my righteous longing
for the moment of your return,
when all creation will be liberated
from every futility in which it now languishes.

THE END OF A MATTER IS BETTER THAN ITS BEGINNING; A PATIENT SPIRIT IS BETTER THAN A PROUD SPIRIT.
—ECCLESIASTES 7:8

Be present in my waiting, O Lord,
that I might also be present in it
as a Christ-bearer to those before and behind me,
who also wait.

Amen.

- Consider the object of your waiting—that moment you desire or thing you seek to obtain. How much weight have you asked it to bear in your life? How much hope and security have you invested in it? Spend time reflecting on those things in your life that seem dependent on its fulfillment.

- Consider other seasons of waiting in your life. How has the Lord met you in the in-between? How might you work to stay open to the Lord's presence here again?

- Reflect on the slow work of God in your life and in the life of the world. How might this waiting serve to form you into a nearer image of the Lord?

RESPONSIVE PRAYER:

POETRY READING: ECCLESIASTES 7:8–9
PROSE READING: EPHESIANS 4:20–32

If my heart were more content in you, O Lord,
I would be less inclined to rage at others.

Let me gauge by the knot in my gut,
the poverty of my own understanding
of the grace that I have received
from a God who, loving me,
    chose rather to receive wounds
    than to give them.

Take from me my self-righteousness,
and my ego-driven demands for respect.
Overthrow the tyranny of my anger, O Lord,
and in its place establish a better vision
of your throne, your kingdom, and your peace.

Amen.

AN ENTRY ON

Dealing Redemptively with Anger

FROM "A LITURGY FOR EXPERIENCING ROAD RAGE"

THEREFORE, PUTTING AWAY LYING, SPEAK THE TRUTH, EACH ONE TO HIS NEIGHBOR, BECAUSE WE ARE MEMBERS OF ONE ANOTHER. BE ANGRY AND DO NOT SIN. DON'T LET THE SUN GO DOWN ON YOUR ANGER, AND DON'T GIVE THE DEVIL AN OPPORTUNITY.
—EPHESIANS 4:25–27

- Reflect on moments in Christ's life when he chose to receive wounds rather than to give them. Do any of those circumstances mirror your own in this moment? How might the life of the Messiah—who showed anger, but did not sin—guide your own reactions and decisions right now?

- Consider ways in which your anger in this moment might rise from self-righteousness and ego-driven demands for respect. How might you pray for the Lord to reshape your heart?

- How might patience towards the end of this matter help guide your heart to a holy anger that does not sin? How might you keep the devil from claiming a foothold here?

RESPONSIVE PRAYER:

AN ENTRY ON

Stewarding Daily Tasks

FROM "A LITURGY FOR DOMESTIC DAYS"

WHOEVER IS FAITHFUL IN VERY LITTLE IS ALSO FAITHFUL IN MUCH, AND WHOEVER IS UNRIGHTEOUS IN VERY LITTLE IS ALSO UNRIGHTEOUS IN MUCH. SO IF YOU HAVE NOT BEEN FAITHFUL WITH WORLDLY WEALTH, WHO WILL TRUST YOU WITH WHAT IS GENUINE? AND IF YOU HAVE NOT BEEN FAITHFUL WITH WHAT BELONGS TO SOMEONE ELSE, WHO WILL GIVE YOU WHAT IS YOUR OWN?
—LUKE 16:10–12

POETRY READING: PSALM 1
PROSE READING: LUKE 16:1–12

Many are the things that must be daily done.
Meet me therefore, O Lord,
in the doing of the small, repetitive tasks.

High King of Heaven,
you showed yourself among us
as the servant of all, speaking stories
of a kingdom to come, a kingdom in which
those who spend themselves for love, even in the
humblest of services, will not be forgotten,
but whose every service lovingly rendered
will be seen from that far vantage
as the planting of a precious seed
blooming into eternity.

And so I offer this small service to you, O Lord,
for you make no distinction between
  those acts that bring a person
  the wide praise of their peers
and those unmarked acts
  that are accomplished in a quiet obedience
  without accolade.
You see instead the heart, the love,
and the faithful stewardship
of all labors, great and small.

And so, in your loving presence,
I undertake this task.

Amen.

- Consider the frustrations you meet as you go about ordinary tasks. What keeps you from perceiving the holiness of these moments? How might you better recognize the presence of God in the midst of these labors?

- If the one faithful over little is also faithful over much, what is the much over which you desire to be faithful? What are the true riches you are striving to steward?

- Consider the call to meditate on the law of the Lord day and night. How might your ordinary, daily tasks serve also as a way to delight in the Word of the Lord consistently, that your daily labors might bear fruit in due season?

RESPONSIVE PRAYER:

AN ENTRY ON

Faithfulness in Work

FROM "A LITURGY FOR ONE WHO IS EMPLOYED"

POETRY READING: PROVERBS 16:1–3
PROSE READING: PHILIPPIANS 2:1–16

O Christ who supplies my every need,
I praise you for all provisions
and for the means by which they are provided.

Let me work and serve in this position
with mindfulness, creativity, and kindness,
  loving you well by loving
  all whom I encounter here.

Grant me therefore the patience
to listen to others,
the humility to learn from them,
the compassion to consider their needs
as my own,
and the grace to wear well in this place
the name of my Lord,
remembering that I arrive here each day
as an emissary of your kingdom.

May my presence here
daily suggest
your presence here.

And may the outworking of the gospel
be always evident in this my work
that my service
might be ever reckoned and received
as service first rendered unto you, O Christ.

Amen.

DO NOTHING OUT OF SELFISH AMBITION OR CONCEIT, BUT IN HUMILITY CONSIDER OTHERS AS MORE IMPORTANT THAN YOURSELVES. EVERYONE SHOULD LOOK NOT TO HIS OWN INTERESTS, BUT RATHER TO THE INTERESTS OF OTHERS.
—PHILIPPIANS 2:3–4

- Reflect on the path that has brought you to this position. What decisions led you here? What acts driven by faith or desire or need? Remember your own story and pay attention to the unfolding "chapters" of your life that have brought you here.

- Consider the challenges you face in this position—tasks, relationships, time, space, energy, etc. What do you love about your work? What frustrates you? What do you dread?

- Consider the humility of Christ who served as a craftsman and manual laborer for many years. How might his posture towards his work on earth inform your own?

RESPONSIVE PRAYER:

AN ENTRY ON

Caring for a Home

FROM "A LITURGY FOR HOME REPAIRS"

POETRY READING: PSALM 127
PROSE READING: MATTHEW 7:24–29

For the blessings of this dwelling,
I give you thanks, O Lord,
acknowledging that all provision
is your provision.

This place is a gift.
The sharing of life within these walls is a gift.

Give grace therefore that I might now
perform the task before me,
not in grudging irritation,
but in gentleness and generosity of spirit,
as a caretaker of your blessings,
and as an act of loving service
to all family, friends, or strangers
who will shelter here or enjoy
fellowship beneath this roof.

Guide my hands in these endeavors, O Lord,
and yet even more, I pray that you would shape
my heart in the doing of them, that as I labor
to repair this dwelling, you would be ever at
work within me, your Spirit
making me an ever more fit habitation
for the indwelling Christ,
and a truer citizen
of the coming kingdom.

Amen.

UNLESS THE LORD BUILDS A HOUSE, ITS BUILDERS LABOR OVER IT IN VAIN; UNLESS THE LORD WATCHES OVER A CITY, THE WATCHMAN STAYS ALERT IN VAIN.
—PSALM 127:1

- Consider the home in which you live and the story of your coming to live there. Remember the provision of the Lord. Remember also surprising, significant, and ordinary moments you have spent in your own home—either alone or with others. How has this place become a holy sanctuary in your life, where the Lord dwells with you?

- Consider the tasks necessary to care for this space. What tasks might you do better? How might you care more creatively for the space? How might you make it more beautiful, more meaningful, or more personally reflective of the eternal longings of the people who inhabit it?

- Consider the parable of the wise and foolish homeowners. How might your physical home reflect—in style, decorations, space, habits, meals, conversations, etc.—the spiritual firm foundation on which it has been built?

RESPONSIVE PRAYER:

AN ENTRY ON

Engaging in a Creative Act

FROM "A LITURGY FOR THOSE WHO WORK IN WOOD & STONE & METAL & CLAY"

POETRY READING: PROVERBS 22:29
PROSE READING: 1 THESSALONIANS 4:9–12

I am here to rehearse the New Creation
in the making of this thing.

Breathe, O God, into my lifeless works
that they might somehow hold
in their feeble forms
such angles and fragments and rumors
of the fire of the glory
that is already made ready and waiting
to burst forth from the seams of
creation's old garment—
when you but speak the word.

So now, Creator Spirit, unto that day,
quicken my hands; enliven my imagination.
Mediate my labor; offer inspiration.
With intention, in this shaping, may I love well
those who in the end will benefit by the thing
well-made and useful for their journey.

And so may the thing I here create,
even in its imperfection,
yet be an object bearing witness to the promise
that all things will be made new, a firstfruits
offering to you, from my own hand.

Amen.

BUT WE ENCOURAGE YOU, BROTHERS AND SISTERS, TO DO THIS EVEN MORE, TO SEEK TO LEAD A QUIET LIFE, TO MIND YOUR OWN BUSINESS, AND TO WORK WITH YOUR OWN HANDS, AS WE COMMANDED YOU, SO THAT YOU MAY BEHAVE PROPERLY IN THE PRESENCE OF OUTSIDERS AND NOT BE DEPENDENT ON ANYONE.
—1 THESSALONIANS 4:10B–12

- Reflect on your own journey as one who—made in the image of a creative God—also creates. What has led you here? Who inspired you? What are the things you love and desire to bring forth in the world that have encouraged you to sharpen your skill?

- Reflect also on the raw materials of your craft. God created all matter, ordered it, and pronounced it good. What implications does this have for your own relationship to your materials, tools, and creative processes today?

- What might it mean to "rehearse the new creation?" Is this a principle that extends beyond the creation of art and physical objects? In what other spheres of your life might you also purposefully engage in "rehearsing the new creation?"

RESPONSIVE PRAYER:

AN ENTRY ON

Serving Others

FROM "A LITURGY FOR WAITERS & WAITRESSES"

POETRY READING: ISAIAH 58:6–12
PROSE READING: COLOSSIANS 3:23–24

Give grace this day, O Lord.
I will probably need it.

Some will receive my services
gratefully, engaging me with a cheerful
friendliness and making a point
to show their thankfulness.
What a joy it is to serve them!

But others will make my day difficult,
going out of their ways to be
punitive and demeaning,
meeting any kindness with rebuff,
treating me like an object,
taking out on me whatever
frustrations or disappointments
gnaw at their hearts.

Give me your grace to lavish upon
even the rude and ungrateful, that
I would learn to imitate your
constant mercies and your prodigal love
relentlessly extended even to my own
inconstant heart, O my king.
Let me serve joyfully,
knowing that every
act of service offered in your name
is received by you.

Amen.

WHATEVER YOU DO, DO IT FROM THE HEART, AS SOMETHING DONE FOR THE LORD AND NOT FOR PEOPLE, KNOWING THAT YOU WILL RECEIVE THE REWARD OF AN INHERITANCE FROM THE LORD. YOU SERVE THE LORD CHRIST.
—COLOSSIANS 3:23–24

- Consider various times others have served you and the differences in their posture, demeanor, and tone toward you. Who has served you in a way you want to serve others?

- Consider the theme of compassion in scripture, moving through the Old Testament and taking human shape in the person of Christ. What scriptural stories of compassion and service shape your own?

- Reflect on the truth that you are serving the Lord Christ today in each face you see. How might you keep that idea present in your mind as you labor? How might this truth enable you to serve others, regardless of their immediate responses?

RESPONSIVE PRAYER:

POETRY READING: PROVERBS 9:7–12
PROSE READING: MARK 6:30–34

May I learn to love learning, O Lord,
for the world is yours,
and all things in it speak
—each in their way—of you.

All knowledge is your knowledge.
All wisdom your wisdom.
Therefore, as I apply myself to learning,
may I be mindful that all created things
are your creative expression, that all stories
are held within your greater story,
and that all disciplines of order and design
are a chasing after your thoughts—
so that greater mastery of these subjects
will yield ever greater knowledge of the
symmetry and wonder of your ways.

Give me a deepening knowledge of truth and
a finer discernment of the ideas I encounter
in my studies. Guard my mind always against
error, and guard also my heart against
the temptation to compare my own
performance to the work of my peers,
and so to fall into either of the twin traps
of shame or pride.

Lead me to truth.
Shape me for your service.

Amen.

AN ENTRY ON

Preparing the Heart & Mind for Learning

FROM "A LITURGY FOR STUDENTS & SCHOLARS"

INSTRUCT THE WISE,
AND HE WILL BE WISER STILL;
TEACH THE RIGHTEOUS,
AND HE WILL LEARN MORE.
—PROVERBS 9:9

- Consider what it means to be teachable—open to rebuke, receptive to wisdom. Which people in your life have modeled this for you? In whose footsteps do you follow as you seek to learn well?

- Consider the object of your studies. What is its value to you? What makes it worth the time, effort, and demand required to learn? Are you able to approach the subject from a posture of humility?

- Consider the teaching of Christ. Why might his compassion for the people find expression in a desire to teach them—a desire for them to learn? Consider the connection between compassion and the teaching of truth.

RESPONSIVE PRAYER:

AN ENTRY ON

Abiding in Christ

FROM "A LITURGY FOR THE RITUAL OF MORNING COFFEE"

"REMAIN IN ME, AND I IN YOU. JUST AS A BRANCH IS UNABLE TO PRODUCE FRUIT BY ITSELF UNLESS IT REMAINS ON THE VINE, NEITHER CAN YOU UNLESS YOU REMAIN IN ME. I AM THE VINE; YOU ARE THE BRANCHES. THE ONE WHO REMAINS IN ME AND I IN HIM PRODUCES MUCH FRUIT, BECAUSE YOU CAN DO NOTHING WITHOUT ME."
—JOHN 15:4–5

POETRY READING: PSALM 46
PROSE READING: JOHN 15:1–17

Meet me, O Christ,
 in this stillness
Move me, O Spirit,
 to quiet my heart.
Mend me, O Father,
 from yesterday's harms.

From the discords of yesterday,
 resurrect my peace.
From the discouragements of yesterday,
 resurrect my hope.
From the weariness of yesterday,
 resurrect my strength.
From the doubts of yesterday,
 resurrect my faith.
From the wounds of yesterday,
 resurrect my love.

Let me be ever
aware of my need,
 and awake

to your grace,
O Lord.

Amen.

- What do you feel is keeping you from abiding in Christ in this moment? What fears? What distractions? What burdens? What pride? Attempt to put words around these barriers and, in naming them, pray that the Lord might help you push them aside.

- With as many barriers cleared away as possible, what might it mean now to reside here, open and known, awake to grace?

- Consider how you might help others practice the presence of God. How might your own life become to those around you a more gracious invitation to rest in God and abide in Christ?

RESPONSIVE PRAYER:

AN ENTRY ON

Leading Others

FROM "A LITURGY FOR THOSE WHO EMPLOY OTHERS"

ABOVE ALL, PUT ON LOVE, WHICH IS THE PERFECT BOND OF UNITY. AND LET THE PEACE OF CHRIST, TO WHICH YOU WERE ALSO CALLED IN ONE BODY, RULE YOUR HEARTS. AND BE THANKFUL.
—COLOSSIANS 3:14–15

POETRY READING: ISAIAH 42:15–16
PROSE READING: COLOSSIANS 3:1–15

Teach me each day the way of Christ—
how better to serve those I would lead.

Give me wisdom and mercy in my dealings.
May I be patient, and gracious,
and slow to anger, recognizing always
your image within those I lead.

May I trust first in you as my provision,
that I might relate to others
not as tools and commodities,
but as fellow pilgrims and fellow beggars,
desperate for divine love.

May those who follow my lead here do so with
 a sense of peace
 and purpose
 and calm,
with a sense that they are valued
and respected and appreciated.
and may my dealings with them be
a steady witness and invitation,
beckoning each to respond more fully
to the call of your Spirit.

O Lord, be present in this place.
Be at work in our work.

Amen.

- What might it mean for your leadership to bear witness to the call of the Spirit? How might the environment you create, your delegation of tasks, your communication, or any other element of your work become a better conduit of divine love expressed to those you lead?

- Consider any ways in which your exercise of leadership might distinguish you from those you lead in ways that are harmful, unloving, or simply untrue. How might you better lead from humility?

- Consider how Jesus interacted with his disciples. How might you, in your own context, lead in a similar way, seeking to show the same presence, kindness, and direction?

RESPONSIVE PRAYER:

AN ENTRY ON

Seasons of Rest

FROM "A LITURGY FOR LEAVING ON HOLIDAY"

FOR THE LORD GOD, THE HOLY ONE OF ISRAEL, HAS SAID: "YOU WILL BE DELIVERED BY RETURNING AND RESTING; YOUR STRENGTH WILL LIE IN QUIET CONFIDENCE . . ."
—ISAIAH 30:15A

POETRY READING: ISAIAH 30:15–29
PROSE READING: MARK 2:23–28

O Christ Our Sabbath,
You have fashioned us to function best
in rhyming lines of work and rest;
our relaxations and recreations
like unspoken invitations
to that still greater holiday to come.

Bless now, O Lord,
this happy foretaste of that good end!

As you called your disciples
to come away with you,
retreating from the crush of crowds,
pausing in their long work,
simply to rest, to reflect, to enjoy your company,
your words, your conversation, to enjoy
their fellowship with one another,

so help me also, in this time,
to carve out spaces merely to be,
    to be with you,
    to be refreshed.

Bless also my eventual transition from rest to work,
that I might return as one who has been revived,
with strength renewed to shoulder once more
the meaningful labor assigned to me
in this season.

Amen.

- Consider your hopes for this time of rest. Are you approaching it with specific goals in mind? What tasks, obligations, or situations are you seeking rest from? And what or whom are you seeking your rest in? Consider expectations, fears, and desires you bring to this season.

- How might the words of Christ that "The Sabbath was made for man, not man for the Sabbath" apply to your time of rest? How might understanding this lead to deeper rest for you during this time?

- Consider for a moment your pending return to daily labors. What concerns do you have coming back from this season of rest? What might make the re-entry difficult?

RESPONSIVE PRAYER:

AN ENTRY ON

Speaking or Performing in Public

FROM "A LITURGY BEFORE TAKING THE STAGE"

POETRY READING: PSALM 147
PROSE READING: MATTHEW 14:13–21

What have I to offer here
that might sustain the souls of others?
Alone I have little more to show

than my own pride and insecurity, my craving
for praise, and my fear of rejection.

Meet me amidst the wreckage
of my ego and my woundedness,
and through me give what I alone cannot.

I offer now these incomplete
and insufficient provisions,
remembering how you, in your days among us,
twice blessed inadequate offerings,
fashioning them into miraculous feasts
that would sustain crowds in their hard journeys.

I pray that you would likewise
receive and bless and multiply
my own meager gifts, Jesus,
for the benefit of all who have gathered here.

Take this tiny heap of my talents
and my brokenness alike,
this jumble of what is best and worst in me,
and meld it to the greater work of your Spirit,
using each facet as you will.

Amen.

HE IS NOT IMPRESSED BY THE STRENGTH OF A HORSE;
HE DOES NOT VALUE THE POWER OF A WARRIOR.
THE LORD VALUES THOSE WHO FEAR HIM,
THOSE WHO PUT THEIR HOPE IN HIS FAITHFUL LOVE.
—PSALM 147:10–11

- Reflect on the journey that has led you to this moment. In what other moments—guiding you to this one—have you met God's presence and kindness? How might you then trust that the Lord's presence and kindness will be manifest here as well?

- Consider those things in which the Lord delights. How might you prepare yourself better for this moment by focusing upon God's sources of joy and not your own pleasures or those of the world?

- Consider the story of Jesus feeding the crowds. How might the accounts of the disciples offering their insufficient gifts to Jesus, then receiving them back from his hand multiplied and made sufficient to meet the needs of others serve as a helpful beginning for you, as you intend to serve? How might an awareness of this pattern free you to better love your audience through the service you offer them?

RESPONSIVE PRAYER:

AN ENTRY ON

Partings & Goodbyes

FROM "A LITURGY FOR LEAVINGS"

POETRY READING: ECCLESIASTES 3:1–8
PROSE READING: HEBREWS 10:23–25

Thank you, O God,
that we do not walk this road alone,
but that this journey towards eternity
and toward your heart has been, from the
beginning, one that you ordained we should
undertake in the glad and good company
of our fellow pilgrims.

O Lord, make us ever mindful of one another
unto the end that we would labor in the
days to come as those who would tend and
encourage the stories of those around us by
prayer and friendship and thoughtfulness and
conversation, affirming and sharpening and
amplifying one another's good works, unto the
end that your body would be built up, and that
your kingdom would be more fully realized
in this world.

By your Spirit, O Christ,
make us faithful in the meanwhile,
as we go out to labor in the diverse fields
to which you have assigned us,
laboring unto that better meeting,
and unto that new-made world,
that is yet promised, and that has already begun.

O Spirit of God, be as present in our parting
as you were in our gathering.

Amen.

AND LET US CONSIDER ONE ANOTHER IN ORDER TO PROVOKE LOVE AND GOOD WORKS, NOT NEGLECTING TO GATHER TOGETHER, AS SOME ARE IN THE HABIT OF DOING, BUT ENCOURAGING EACH OTHER, AND ALL THE MORE AS YOU SEE THE DAY APPROACHING.
—HEBREWS 10:24–25

- Consider the life you have shared with those from whom you are being parted. Spend time and words in gratitude for what has been true of your journey together and for the holy moments you have shared.

- Consider the fears and concerns you bring to this leaving. What worries you about this parting? What disquiet in this might you bring to the Lord—one who is not leaving you and never will?

- What might it look like to encourage one another all the more after this leaving, now that you must refrain from meeting together?

RESPONSIVE PRAYER:

AN ENTRY FOR

Blessing a Space

FROM "A LITURGY FOR MOVING INTO A NEW HOME"

POETRY READING: PSALM 5: 11–12
PROSE READING: 2 CORINTHIANS 5:1–10

We thank you for this space,
O Lord, for the shelter it will provide, for the
moments of life that will be shared within it.

Dwell with us in this place, O Lord.
Dwell among us in these spaces, in these rooms.

May your Spirit inhabit this space,
making of it a sanctuary
where hearts and lives are knit together,
where bonds of love are strengthened,
where mercy is learned and practiced.

May this be a place of knowing
and of being known,
a place of shared tears and laughter;
a place where forgiveness is easily asked
and granted, and wounds are quickly healed;
a place of meaningful conversation,
of words not left unsaid;
a place of joining, of becoming,
of creating, and reflecting;
a place where our diverse gifts
are named and appreciated;
where we learn to serve one another
and to serve our neighbors as well;
a place where our stories are forever twined
by true affections.

Amen.

FOR WE KNOW THAT IF OUR EARTHLY TENT WE LIVE IN IS DESTROYED, WE HAVE A BUILDING FROM GOD, AN ETERNAL DWELLING IN THE HEAVENS, NOT MADE WITH HANDS.
—2 CORINTHIANS 5:1

- As you embark on a new season within this space, take a moment to mark the characteristics of this beginning. What are the delights and joys? Are there any losses, any griefs you bring to it?

- Consider the eternal dwelling from God awaiting us in the renewed creation, and the temple space that we ourselves are for his Spirit dwelling on earth. How might reflection on these spiritual spaces shape the way you steward this earthly space?

- Ponder the physical possibilities for this space—design, decor, furniture, lighting, resources, art, etc. How might this space, and your stewardship of its small details, be used to better reflect the Kingdom of God on earth?

RESPONSIVE PRAYER:

AN ENTRY ON

Seasons of Insomnia & Exhaustion

FROM "A LITURGY FOR THOSE WHO CANNOT SLEEP"

POETRY READING: PSALM 6
PROSE READING: EXODUS 33:12–14

O Christ Who Is My Rest,
this tension of body,
and racing of mind,
and clamoring of heart
afford me no peace in this night.

Unable to sleep I would yet
make use of my restlessness, O Lord.
Amidst doubt, anxiety, uncertainty,
I would learn to practice a more constant
awareness of your presence, directing
heart and thought and petition to you.

Lay your hand upon my brow, O Lord,
and bid me calm. Even in haggard sleeplessness,
let me yet recognize my utter dependence
upon you, remembering that you are with me
whether I sleep or not.

AND [THE LORD] REPLIED, "MY PRESENCE WILL GO WITH YOU, AND I WILL GIVE YOU REST."
—EXODUS 33:14

Even if mind or body refuse their rest,
still let my soul take its repose
in the enfolding comfort of your presence,
my head reclined against your breast, hearing
the deep music of your heartbeat.
Waking or sleeping, O Lord,
be this night my rest,
and on the morrow, my strength.

Amen.

- The limits of our human bodies are painfully evident in seasons of exhaustion. Meanwhile, we are reminded that we are beautifully and wonderfully made. As you are deeply aware of your limits in this season, what are ways God has provided you with strength for enduring?

- How might you be reminded of the presence of God in this moment of tension? Where does he show himself in these difficult seasons? In what ways does he, even now, offer you rest?

- Consider times in which you feel most restful in the presence of God—listening to music, reading, writing, walking, stepping outside, etc. How might it be beneficial to engage in one of these activities when faced with sleeplessness?

RESPONSIVE PRAYER:

POETRY READING: PSALM 119:105–112
PROSE READING: GENESIS 12:1–3

How marvelous it is, O Lord,
that you contemplated each of us
before we were made!

How marvelous that you considered and created us, decreeing the very time and place that each of us should enter the world to live out our own part of your grand story. And so I celebrate today the unique place of ____________ in the epic tale of redemption.

You have created each of us, O Lord, to bear your image in unique expression, reflecting a facet of your glory in a way that no other person in all of history will, so that by knowing one another we might also know you better. And so I celebrate and honor your image, O God, uniquely reflected in the life and in the personhood of ____________.

Bless this, your child. May they know the comfort of your presence, the certainty of your purpose, and the consolation of your love at work in their life.

Grant them
    wisdom, maturity,
    vision, and passion
in increasing measure, that they might be an instrument well-honed for the building of your kingdom.

Amen.

AN ENTRY FOR

Blessing a Person

FROM "A LITURGY FOR THE MARKING OF BIRTHDAYS"

"THE LORD BLESS YOU
AND KEEP YOU;
THE LORD MAKE HIS FACE
SHINE ON YOU
AND BE GRACIOUS TO YOU;
THE LORD TURN HIS
FACE TOWARD YOU
AND GIVE YOU PEACE."
—NUMBERS 6:24–26

- What blessings have come from this person's presence in your life? Give thanks to God for these specific things.

- What are the special gifts God has given this person to uniquely serve his kingdom? How can you encourage them in the development and use of those gifts?

- What are the needs of this person, and how can you pray for them now and in the future?

RESPONSIVE PRAYER:

AN ENTRY ON

Seasons of Financial Worry

FROM "A LITURGY FOR THE PAYING OF BILLS"

POETRY READING: PSALM 1
PROSE READING: HEBREWS 13:1–6

O God Who Does Provide
All Things Necessary for Our Lives,
be present with me now.

For there is little in this life that will so starkly
reveal my insecurities and my struggle to trust
your tender care as will the state of my heart
when I consider the state of my finances—
when I am anxious about money, O Lord,
I can slip so easily into the downward spiral
of believing that simply having more of it
would guarantee my security.

As if my security could ever rest anywhere
outside of you, O God.
So guard my heart against that lie.
Let me learn to view money and all material
things as an arena in which to learn and practice
a more faithful stewardship,
and as a means by which to invest in things
eternal—but never as ends in themselves.

YOU CARE FOR THE LAND AND WATER IT; YOU ENRICH IT ABUNDANTLY. THE STREAMS OF GOD ARE FILLED WITH WATER TO PROVIDE THE PEOPLE WITH GRAIN, FOR SO YOU HAVE ORDAINED IT.
—PSALM 65:9

Do not abandon me to my anxieties over
finances, O Lord, but use those worries to
turn my heart and thoughts to you—
then teach me both a greater contentment
and a greater confidence in
your constant care.

Amen.

- Reflect on the lack of security you feel right now. Be specific in your concerns. How are you lacking both contentment and confidence in the Lord's care?

- Consider the images of provision in scripture for God's people. How might your worry be calmed by reshaping your understanding of prosperity?

- Financial concerns will likely return again. How can you keep yourself from the downward spiral of trusting in material wealth for assurance and contentment in the future?

RESPONSIVE PRAYER:

AN ENTRY ON

Uncomfortable Conversations

FROM "A LITURGY FOR THOSE WHO FEEL AWKWARD IN SOCIAL GATHERINGS"

LET YOUR CONVERSATION
BE ALWAYS FULL OF GRACE,
SEASONED WITH SALT, SO THAT
YOU MAY KNOW HOW
TO ANSWER EVERYONE.
—COLOSSIANS 4:6

POETRY READING: PSALM 133
PROSE READING: COLOSSIANS 4:2–6

I know that you have not called me, O Lord,

to insulate my heart from others,
or from the discomfort I might feel
in the presence of acquaintances and strangers.

You have called me instead
to learn to love by my small actions
and choices, those whose paths I cross,
moment to moment, in all settings.

Give me grace therefore, O God,
to love others, to move toward them
when my instinct is to run.

Quell my discomfort enough that I might consider
with true compassion the needs of
another human being.

Then let me consciously,
and as an act of love and choosing to love,
move toward that person.
Let your grace compel my movements.

In such moments, let me think less of myself
and my own awkwardness.
Let me think more of others,
and let me think more of you.

Amen.

- Take a moment to reflect on the interaction you are anticipating. What concerns do you carry? What has brought about your desire to run from this?

- Consider what compassion looks like in this situation. What might you say or do differently out of a choice to love—a choice to run towards and not away from? How might you "season your speech with salt?"

- Consider God's design for community and the Scriptural blessing on unity. How might you, even now in what is awkward or uncomfortable, move towards meaningful relationship with another person?

RESPONSIVE PRAYER:

AN ENTRY ON

Contentment in the Midst of Coveting

FROM "A LITURGY FOR THOSE WHO COVET THE LATEST TECHNOLOGY"

POETRY READING: PROVERBS 15:27
PROSE READING: 1 TIMOTHY 6:3–20

Content my soul in you, O Christ,
who alone are sufficient to my longings.

When my heart is beset by wheedling desire
for what it does not have,
remind me, sweet Jesus, that

I have no right to a thing simply because it
exists. The perpetual allure of the new
does not negate the call to faithfully steward
those resources you have temporarily
entrusted to my keeping.

I would be your trusted servant
at liberty to employ and to enjoy
all things at my disposal,
without being owned by any of them.

Content my soul therefore in you, O Christ,
who alone are sufficient to my longings.

Amen.

BUT GODLINESS WITH CONTENTMENT IS GREAT GAIN. FOR WE BROUGHT NOTHING INTO THE WORLD, AND WE CAN TAKE NOTHING OUT OF IT.
—1 TIMOTHY 6:6–7

- Reflect on the desire you have. Why do you believe this thing ought to be yours? Is there a disordered hope or priority at the root of this desire? Can you identify it?

- Consider the call to steward what you already have. How might you fight the temptation to covet by moving more faithfully towards stewardship? Give specific details on what this might look like in your life, as you tend what has been entrusted to you.

- What might the apostle mean in his call to be rich in good works? How might renewing your understanding of true wealth aid in the fight against coveting? What is the right relationship between material things and the eternal Kingdom of God?

RESPONSIVE PRAYER:

POETRY READING: LUKE 1:45–55
PROSE READING: JOHN 1: 1–5

As we prepare our house for the coming
Christmas season, we would also prepare our
hearts for the returning Christ.
You came once for your people,
O Lord, and you will come for us again.

Though there was no room at the inn
to receive you upon your first arrival,
we would prepare you room
    here in our hearts
    and here in our home,
Lord Christ.

As we decorate and celebrate, we do so to mark
the memory of your redemptive movement into
our broken world, O God.

Our wreaths and ribbons and colored lights,
our giving of gifts, our parties with friends—
these have never been ends in themselves.
These are but small ways in which we repeat
that sounding joy first proclaimed by angels
in the skies near Bethlehem.

Now we celebrate your first coming, Immanuel,
even as we long for your return.
O Prince of Peace, our elder brother, return
soon! We miss you so!

Amen.

AN ENTRY ON THE

Christmas Season

FROM "A LITURGY TO MARK THE START OF THE CHRISTMAS SEASON"

IN HIM WAS LIFE, AND THAT LIFE WAS THE LIGHT OF ALL MANKIND. THE LIGHT SHINES IN THE DARKNESS, AND THE DARKNESS HAS NOT OVERCOME IT.
—JOHN 1:4–5

- Consider the ways you have repeated "the sounding joy" in Christmases past. What of these traditions do you wish to bring into this year's celebration? What new traditions or practices might you adopt as you seek to prepare room in your heart and home for the coming king this year?

- Reflect on life between two Advents: the first coming of Christ as an infant, and the second coming of Christ in glory. What might it mean to celebrate one coming while anticipating another?

- Consider Mary's Magnificat. Her song is one of delight in the salvation of her Lord. With the themes of this week's liturgy and Mary's words in mind, craft your own "magnificat" to pray throughout this Christmas season.

RESPONSIVE PRAYER:

AN ENTRY ON

Preparing for a Feast with Friends

FROM "A LITURGY FOR FEASTING WITH FRIENDS"

POETRY READING: PSALM 36:5–9
PROSE READING: EPHESIANS 6:12

In celebrating this feast,
we declare that evil and death,
suffering and loss, sorrows and tears
will not have the final word.

But the joy of fellowship, and the welcome
and comfort of friends new and old,
and the celebration of these blessings of
food and drink and conversation and laughter
are the true evidences of things eternal,
and are the first fruits of that great glad joy
that is to come and that will be unending.

So let our feast this day be joined
to those sure victories secured by Christ.
Let it be to us now a delight, and a glad
foretaste of his eternal kingdom.
Bless us, O Lord, in this feast.

HOW PRICELESS IS YOUR UNFAILING LOVE, O GOD! PEOPLE TAKE REFUGE IN THE SHADOW OF YOUR WINGS. THEY FEAST ON THE ABUNDANCE OF YOUR HOUSE; YOU GIVE THEM DRINK FROM YOUR RIVER OF DELIGHTS.
—PSALM 36:7–8

May this shared meal, and our pleasure in it,
bear witness against the artifice and deceptions
of the prince of the darkness that would blind
this world to hope. May it strike at the root of the lie
that would drain life of meaning, and
the world of joy, and suffering of redemption.

May this feast be an echo of that great
Supper of the Lamb,
a foreshadowing of the great celebration
that awaits the children of God.

- Reflect on the significant feasts in your life—those in the past and those yet to come. What details make them meaningful? What makes them stand apart from ordinary meals?

- Consider Psalm 36. How does feasting, for David, bear witness to the love of God? How is it framed as an act of faithfulness for the righteous?

- Consider the idea of feasting as an act of war, as described in this week's liturgy—bearing witness against deceptions, striking at lies, and declaring a victory already secured. How might this idea shape your feasts—those you attend or those you host?

RESPONSIVE PRAYER:

ALSO AVAILABLE FROM

RABBIT ROOM PRESS

Every Moment Holy, Volume 1

Every Moment Holy, Volume 2: Death, Grief, & Hope

Every Moment Holy, Volume 3: The Work of the People

WWW.EVERYMOMENTHOLY.COM